R AMAZING! ™

We find the amazing in the ordinary everyday with lists, polls and quizzes. Helping us to appreciate, in fun and quirky ways, the world in which we live.

Creating interactive content, R Amazing! is a safe place to explore different topics and share your views.

It is ok to disagree with us regarding who or what we think is amazing! We share our thoughts on our website and in our books to enable debate and discussion.

We encourage the expression of opinions in an appropriate way with an understanding that it is ok for people to have differing views.

R Amazing! debates should be conducted politely and respectfully, ending with an agreement and common ground, even if that is to agree to disagree.

www.r-amazing.com

Cats R Amazing!
Mark 'Markus' Baker & Adam Galvin

Published by R-and-Q.com.
Copyright © 2019 R-and-Q.com

CATS

R AMAZING! ™

www.r-amazing.com/cats/

Adam Galvin and Markus Baker
Creators of R Amazing!

"*Cats choose us;
we don't own them.*"
Kristin Cast

"

*A cat has absolute
emotional honesty:
human beings, for one...*

...reason or another, may hide their feelings, but a cat does not.

Ernest Hemingway

House Cats

Have you ever wondered when cats became domesticated?

It is not exactly clear when cats chose to live in our homes, this is because domestic and wild cats have very similar skeletons. Archaeological records believe cats domesticated themselves around 12,000 years ago. This was revealed when scientists found 30,000 cat mummies in an Egypt boneyard.

Genetic analysis suggests all house cats have descended from the middle eastern wildcat, Felis Sylvestris. The Egyptian's loved their feline friends so much that a person who killed a cat could face the death penalty if found guilty.

We think what happened is that the cats sort of domesticated themselves.

Carlos Driscoll

Street Cat Named Bob

A London street performer and recovering drug addict, James Bowen, discovered a sick cat in his building on his return home. Helping the unidentified cat recover from illness, Bowen named the cat Bob.

Bob began to follow James everywhere. People loved this performing duo and uploaded their photos and videos to social media. Many tourists would visit Covent Garden just to see them busk.

Catching everyone's attention, Bowen shared his story in his book 'The Little Book of Bob: Life Lessons from a Street-Wise Cat'. This was later adapted in a movie named 'A Street Cat Named Bob'.

"Everybody needs a break, everybody deserves that second chance."
James Bowen

DID YOU KNOW?

Cats can rotate their ears
180 degrees because they
have 32 muscles in each
ear compared to the
6 in a human ear.

Source: https://www.cbc.ca/natureofthings/m_features/the-not-so-humble-housecat

The phrase 'domestic cat'
is an oxymoron.

George Will

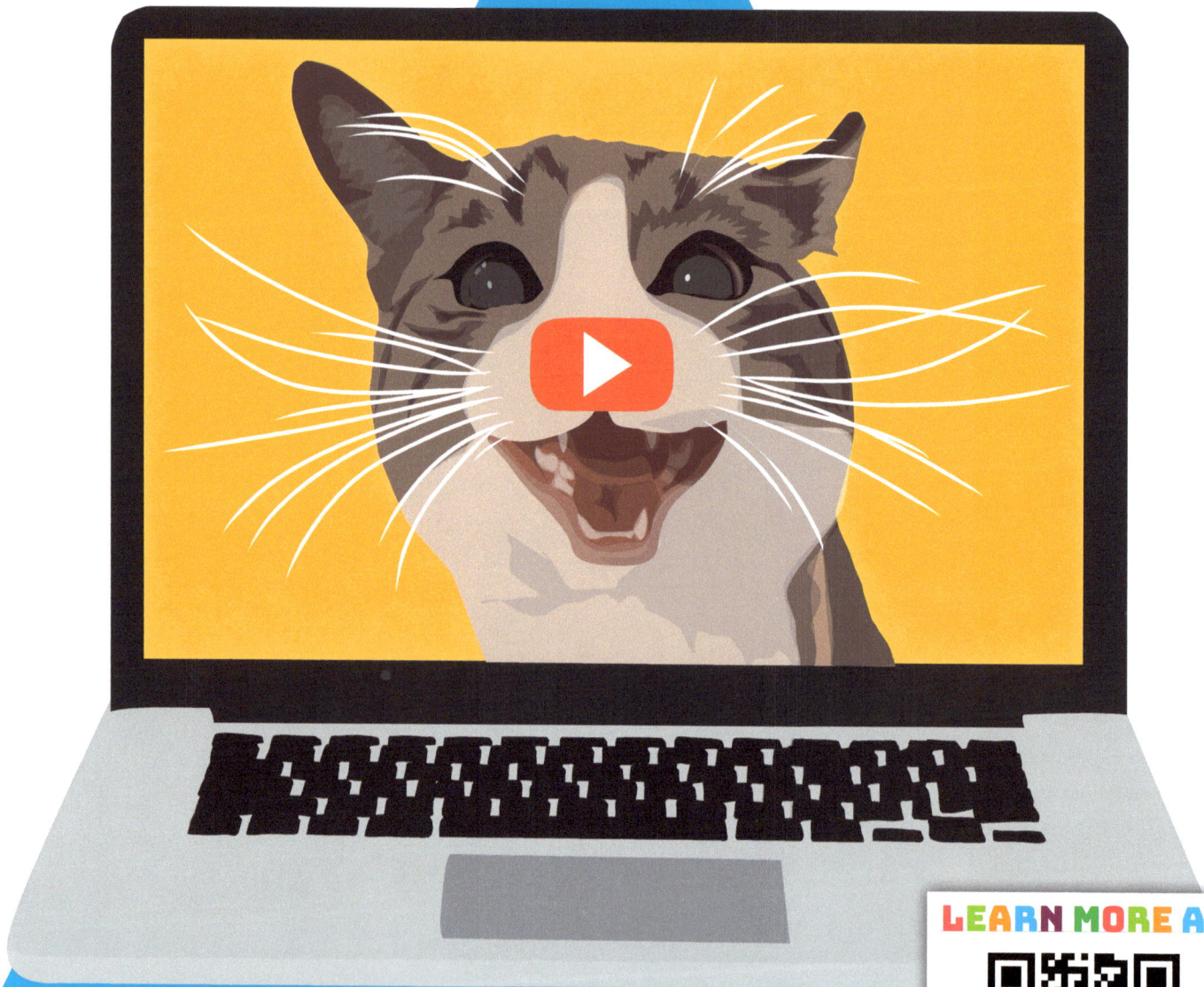

Cat Videos

Have you ever opened a cat video on YouTube and ended up watching many of them?

YouTube has more than two million cat videos which have been watched over 25 billion times. That is an average of around 12,000 views per video.

Why do people watch so many cat videos? A scientific study revealed that they make people happier by relieving stress.

One cat just leads to another.
Ernest Hemingway

LEARN MORE AT

www.r-amazing.com/lil-bub/

Lil Bub

An American celebrity cat named 'Lil Bub' gained over 3 million likes on Facebook. This fragile little cat was adopted when Mike Bridavsky's friend asked him to give her shelter.

Being the runt of the litter with a small jaw and no teeth, Lil Bub's tongue hung out of her mouth giving her a unique physical appearance.

Lil Bub's pictures were first seen on the blog Tumblr in 2011 and later was featured on Reddit. She went on to star in the documentary 'Lil Bub and Friends' that won the best feature film at the 2013 Tribeca Film Festival.

> *She looked like Gizmo from Gremlins, only cuter, and real. Naturally, I rushed over to meet her.*
> Mike Bridavsky

"

In ancient times cats were
worshipped as gods; they
have not forgotten this.

Terry Pratchett

DID YOU KNOW?

Cats learn by being rewarded with positive reinforcement. They do not understand punishment. We must praise a cat if we want a specific behaviour.

Cat's Meow

Facial expressions, body language and scent are the ways adult cats communicate with each other. Cats even greet one another by touching noses to find out what they have each been up to.

Learning that humans do not respond to their usual communication, cats chose to use the same 'Meow' method they use to talk to kittens.

> *Cats seem to go on the principle that it never does any harm to ask for what you want.*
>
> Joseph Wood Krutch

Rescued Each Other

A kitten was discovered and rescued at the roadside by Danielle Schafer. She named it Kitty.

Five years later, Kitty returned the favour by saving Schafer.

Asleep in her first-floor apartment, Kitty jumped on Danielle to wake her up. Schafer woke to discover flames consuming her apartment. Managing to escape, Kitty was still inside.

Later a firefighter appeared holding her little grey Kitty. This clever cat survived by hiding in the pillows for a few hours to avoid getting consumed by the flames.

> " *The only thing a cat worries about is what's happening right now.* "
> Lloyd Alexander

DID YOU KNOW?

Sir Isaac Newton, the English mathematician, physicist, astronomer, theologian, and author who introduced the world to the understanding of gravity also invented the cat flap.

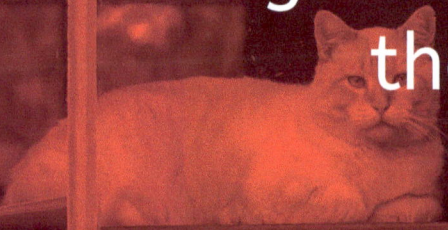

Source: https://coleandmarmalade.com/2018/12/31/25-interesting-facts-about-cats-you-may-not-have-known/

Time spent with cats is never wasted.
Sigmund Freud

Cat's Name

It has been discovered that cats can recognize their name when they are called. A study of house cats concluded that when speaking four different words, including the cat's name. The cat's reaction and behaviour of moving their ears, head, tail or making a noise was clearer when their name was spoken.

Have you noticed how cats move their ears when their names are called?

"

As anyone who has ever been around a cat for any length of time well knows, cats have enormous patience with the limitations of the humankind.

Cleveland Amory

"

Caring Cats

Your cat may love you more than you think. Believe it or not, a cat gets as emotionally attached to you just as much as babies and dogs do.

Cats behaviour has been known to change when their human is poorly. One owner's cat even brought him a tissue when he was sick, something his feline friend had never done before.

Cats can also become clingy when sensing human illness. Upon returning from the hospital one owner noticed her cat following her everywhere and seemed to be much more caring than usual.

I have studied many philosophers and many cats. The wisdom of cats is infinitely superior.

Hippolyte Taine

Cats can work out mathematically the exact place to sit that will cause most inconvenience.

Pam Brown

DID YOU KNOW?

A group of cats is called a clowder. A litter of kittens can also be called a kindle.

Blind Kitten

In constant pain, Carrot, the kitten was discovered on the streets of Prague.

Requiring surgery, Carrot's sore eyes needed to be removed.

Carrot now only sees light and shadows but is free from pain. She is playful and enjoys noisy toys. Her hearing and smelling senses have become more refined. Carrot is a very friendly cat who loves to cuddle humans, other felines and even dogs.

" *A meow massages the heart.*
Stuart McMillan "

The Adventurous Cat

George the cat is a social media star for being very adventurous. Loving to catch free rides on buses and trains around Scotland, this cat travels miles from his home.

When George went missing for four days, his Facebook followers campaigned to help find him. He was eventually discovered 14 miles away, near Loch Lomond.

Once George was caught trying to join a school bus trip to a Safari and Adventure Park in Stirling. Maybe George was planning to visit his larger cousins, Tiger and Lion?

"
*Cats are inquisitive,
but hate to admit it.*
Mason Cooley
"

DID YOU KNOW?

A male cat is generally referred to as a 'Tom Cat' whereas a female cat is known as a 'Molly Cat'.

Source: https://coleandmarmalade.com/2018/12/31/25-interesting-facts-about-cats-you-may-not-have-known/

Human beings are drawn to cats because they are all we are not — self-contained, elegant in everything they do, relaxed, assured, glad of company, yet still possessing secret lives

Pam Brown

Secret Lives

Have you ever wondered what your cat does all day?

To help answer that very question, in 2012, and in collaboration with the Royal Veterinary College the BBC created the TV program 'Horizon: The Secret Life of the Cat'

For one whole week, 50 cats were tracked using GPS and micro cameras.

Other than learning that cat's sleep a lot, anywhere between 16 and 20 hours per day! The main discoveries were that cats do not wander far from home. They sneak into neighbours' houses at night to pinch food. A researcher for the programme, Dr John Bradshaw, also suggested that he felt cats actually own the owners, and not the other way round as humans may sometimes believe.

Like all pure creatures,
cats are practical.
William S. Burroughs

*If cats could talk,
they wouldn't.*

Nan Porter

DID YOU KNOW?

A cat's nose is as individual
to them as a fingerprint
is to a human.

My picture of the most amazing cat in the world!

The most amazing cat in the world is

I love it when this amazing cat...

....

....

....

....

....

....

This cat is amazing because...

....

....

....

....

MORE BOOKS BY R&Q

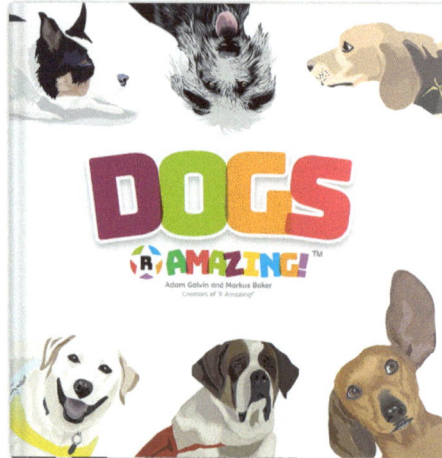

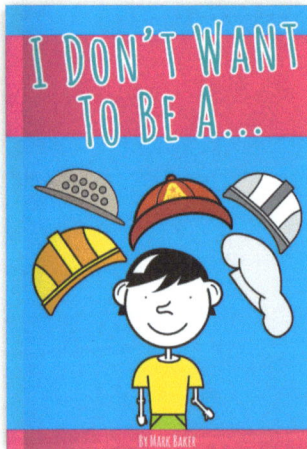

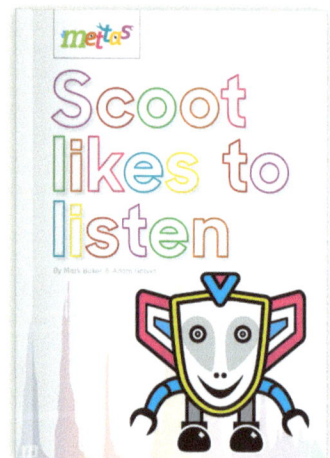

DOOR KNOB FOR A NOSE

DOGS R AMAZING!
Adam Galvin and Markus Baker
Creators of 'R Amazing!'

COOL AS duck
BY MARK BAKER

I DON'T WANT TO BE A...
BY MARK BAKER

THIS BOOK NEVER ENDS...
...it keeps looping round and round until somebody says "PLEASE STOP READING NOW!"
Who is going to give up first? The grown up or the child because...
By Mark Baker

mettas
Scoot likes to listen
By Mark Baker & Adam Galvin

www.ingramcontent.com/pod-product-compliance
Lightning Source LLC
Chambersburg PA
CBHW041546040426
42447CB00002B/63